The Door Left Ajar

A Journey Through Love & Time

Hinal Rathod

Made with ❤ on the BookLeaf Publishing Platform

www.bookleafpub.in

www.bookleafpub.com

Dedication

To the love that arrived like a whisper,
the love that left without a sound
and the love that still lingers in the spaces between.

To the echoes of footsteps that never returned,
the letters never sent
and the doors left slightly open—
not for those who left, but for those who still believe.

To the moments that became memories,
the memories that became stories
and the stories that refuse to end.

This book is for you.

Preface

"Love is not lost in time—it lingers in the echoes, in the letters unsent, in the doors left ajar."

Love and time have always been entwined, moving together like waves on the shore—sometimes gentle, sometimes relentless. Some loves last forever, while others fade like ink on an old letter. Some doors close completely, while others remain slightly open, whispering of possibilities left behind.

The Door Left Ajar: A Journey Through Love & Time is not just a collection of poetry, but a reflection of the emotions we carry, the memories we revisit, and the questions we never quite answer. Each poem is a moment—a flicker of love, loss, longing, or hope— captured in words that linger like echoes of the past.

There are stories we finish and stories we leave unread. There are loves we let go and loves we return to, over and over again. Somewhere in these pages, you may find a piece of your own journey—a letter never sent, a door never fully closed, a feeling that never quite faded.

This book is not meant to tell you how love should be. It

is an invitation to feel, to remember and to wonder: If
love still lingers, will you open the door?

— **Hinal Rathod**

Acknowledgements

No journey is ever taken alone, and this book is no exception. *The Door Left Ajar: A Journey Through Love & Time* was born from moments, emotions and reflections that have shaped me and I am deeply grateful to those who have been a part of this path.

To the ones who have loved me, lost me, found me, or waited for me—this book carries pieces of you. Your presence, even in absence, has left imprints on these pages.

To my family and friends—your unwavering support, encouragement and belief in my words have given me the courage to share this with the world.

To my readers—whether you are here for answers, for nostalgia, or simply to feel something, thank you for stepping into these pages with me. May you find a reflection of your own journey within these words.

And finally, to time itself—the silent witness of love's arrival and departure. You have taught me that some stories end, some continue and some doors are never truly closed.

With gratitude,
Hinal Rathod

1. The First Page

Once, I wrote your name in ink,
Folded the letter, let it sink.
If love is real but left unread,
Does it still live, or is it dead?

Every new beginning feels uncertain, like a book with blank pages waiting to be filled. We hesitate before taking the first step, unsure if the words will come together or if the story will make sense. But a page left empty is still a story untold, a love never written, a life waiting to unfold.

2. The Letter Never Sent

Once, I wrote your name in ink,
Folded the letter, let it sink.
If love is real but left unread,
Does it still live, or is it dead?

There are always words left unsaid, messages written but never delivered. They sit in journals, in drafts, in the quiet spaces of the heart. Love does not disappear just because it was never spoken. It lingers in the air, between the spaces where two souls once met, waiting to be acknowledged.

3. The Rusted Key

I found a key in a wooden chest,
A rusted thing, once held with zest.
Is love like this—forgotten, old?
Or does it shine when strong hands hold?

Some doors stay locked for years, not because they cannot be opened, but because we fear what we might find behind them. Old keys rest in forgotten places, holding memories of hands that once held them tightly. Love, like a rusted key, is never truly lost. It only waits for someone brave enough to turn it again.

4. The Mirror's Truth

I look at you, you look at me,
But do we see what's meant to be?
Is love the glass, or love the view?
A question clear, but answers few.

Love is often seen through the lens of longing, of hope, of fear. Mirrors never lie, but sometimes the heart does, painting illusions where truth should be. When we stand before the reflection of our love, do we recognize it for what it truly is, or only for what we wish it to be?

5. The Candle & The Flame

A candle flickers, soft and bright,
Fighting hard against the night.
Does love burn on, or melt away?
Does time decide, or do we stay?

Some flames burn brightly, while others flicker and fade with time. Love, like fire, can bring warmth or leave behind only smoke. Even when the candle has melted away, its glow remains in the dark corners of memory, reminding us that once, there was light.

6. The Dust On Memories

I traced my fingers on old frames,
The laughter there, the whispered names.
If dust can hide what once was true,
Does love remain, or must we choose?

Memories settle like dust in the quiet corners of life, clinging to old photographs, familiar scents and places once visited together. Some people choose to wipe them away, making space for something new. Others let them linger, knowing that even dust can hold the weight of something precious.

7. The Locked Diary

Pages filled with words so deep,
Secrets held, yet none to keep.
If love is hidden, does it die?
Or does it wait with silent sighs?

There are stories we tell and stories we keep locked away. Love sometimes lives in silence, in pages that remain unread, in words too fragile to be spoken aloud. But no lock is forever. Some diaries are meant to be opened, some secrets meant to be shared and some loves meant to be remembered.

8. The Dance We Forgot

Step by step, we learned the tune,
Hands held tight beneath the moon.
But did we move, or stand too still?
Did love fade out, or wait until?

Love is a dance, a rhythm between two hearts moving as one. But sometimes, the music fades and two souls lose their steps. Some find their way back, relearning the melody they once knew, while others step away, knowing that some dances are not meant to last forever.

9. The Clock In The Hall

The ticking hands, they never pause,
They move ahead with unseen laws.
But does love move, or does it wait?
Can hearts keep time, or must they break?

Time moves forward, carrying love with it, changing it, shaping it, sometimes leaving it behind. Some loves grow with time, while others remain frozen in memories. A clock never stops ticking, but some hearts do, holding onto a moment long after it has passed.

10. The Window At Dust

You stood by the window, looking out,
At golden skies, at stars in doubt.
Did you long for me or something more?
Did love stay in, or walk out the door?

Standing by a window, watching the world outside, love can feel both near and distant at the same time. There is a moment before every goodbye where we hesitate, where we wonder if we should stay or go. Some stay, watching the world move on without them. Others step away, leaving the window open just enough for the breeze of what could have been.

11. The Unfinished Letter

I started a note but left it undone,
Some words are heavy, meant for none.
If love is real but left unsaid,
Does it still live, or is it dead?

Some stories do not end because they were never truly meant to. An unfinished letter, a conversation cut short, a love that never got the chance to be spoken into existence. But even in silence, love leaves its mark, lingering in the spaces where words were meant to be.

12. The Ring In The Drawer

A silver band in velvet folds,
A love once bright, now dulled in gold.
Do things hold love, or is it us?
What truly lasts—what earns our trust?

A ring is not just metal; it carries the weight of promises, of memories, of love given and sometimes lost. Some rings remain on fingers, others are tucked away in drawers, hidden but never forgotten. Love does not live in objects, but in the moments they remind us of, in the hands that once held them, in the hearts that once believed they would last forever.

13. The Room Of Whispers

The walls still hear the fights, the sighs,
The love that lived, the long goodbyes.
If walls could speak, what would they say?
Would love return, or slip away?

Walls remember the things we try to forget. A room that once held laughter still carries the sound of it, echoing in the silence left behind. Love, even when it has left the room, lingers in the air, waiting for someone to listen.

14. The Perfume In The Air

The scent of roses, soft yet deep,

A trace of love we chose to keep.

Can something small bring back the past?

Or does it fade like things don't last?

Some scents bring back entire lifetimes in a single breath. A familiar perfume, the scent of rain, a hint of jasmine on the wind—love can return in the smallest of moments. Some chase the scent, longing for what was. Others simply close their eyes and breathe it in, letting the past wrap around them like a warm embrace.

15. The Broken Teacup

A crack runs through its porcelain white,
Yet still, it holds, still, it fights.
Is love the same—though cracked with pain,
Does it still pour, does it remain?

Not everything that is broken is meant to be discarded. A cracked teacup still holds warmth, just as love, even after heartache, can still hold meaning. Some choose to mend what is broken, while others let it go, knowing that even in its fractured state, it was once whole.

16. The Hourglass of Us

Sand slips down, but do we see?
Each grain, a moment lost, set free.
If we could turn it, start once more,
Would love return, like days before?

Time never stops, even when we wish it would. Some moments slip through our fingers, lost forever, while others remain etched in our souls. If given the chance, would we turn the hourglass back to relive the past, or would we simply watch as each grain of sand reminds us that love, once lived, is never truly gone?

17. The Foot Steps In The Hall

I heard them once, but not again,
Footsteps light like summer rain.
Did love walk out, or did it stay?
Is it just quiet, or gone away?

Some footsteps fade, but their presence never truly leaves. The sound of someone who once walked beside us lingers in quiet hallways, in old conversations, in places where love used to live. Love does not always announce its departure. Sometimes, it simply stops walking.

18. The Last Question

If I knocked now upon your door,
Would you open like before?
Or would the past stand in between,
Like ghosts of love we've left unseen?

A knock on the door, a moment of hesitation. Love does not always return the way we expect it to. Some stand frozen, unsure if they are ready to open the door. Others reach for the handle, knowing that love, even when unexpected, is still worth answering.

19. The Open Window

The breeze still moves the curtain's lace,
Like gentle hands, like love's embrace.
If love can drift but not depart,
Does it still breathe inside the heart?

Love, like the wind, cannot always be held. It drifts in and out, leaving behind whispers of what was and what could be. Some close the window, shutting it out forever. Others leave it open, just in case love decides to return.

20. The Candle Burns Low

The wax is soft, the flame is weak,
The light still warm, but can it speak?
If love grows quiet, if love grows dim,
Is it the end—or a new begin?

Not all flames burn forever, but that does not mean they were never real. A candle may melt away, but its light lingers, casting shadows of what once was. Love, too, may change in form, but does it ever truly disappear?

21. The Door Left Ajar

The door is open, just a crack,
A step ahead, no looking back.
Do we walk through, or stay right here?
Does love return—or disappear?

Some doors are never fully closed, not because they cannot be, but because something inside us is still waiting. The choice is always there—to push it open and step into the unknown or to leave it just as it is, a reminder that some endings are not endings at all, just spaces in between.

www.ingramcontent.com/pod-product-compliance
Lightning Source LLC
Chambersburg PA
CBHW071244140726
47996CB00007B/2752